Lottie

Is the hilarious owner of this book.

Thank You
FOR COMING TO
MY PARTY
7
FROM NANCY

~ Fun Challenge ~

Hey, young explorers! Get ready for an awesome adventure filled with lots of giggles and brain teasers!

As you read through these funny jokes, you'll come across tricky riddles. Can you solve them without peeking?

Once you do, you can impress your friends and family by sharing the riddles with them and see if they can solve them too!

1

~ Joke Telling Tips ~

Practice the joke by saying it out loud to yourself.

Remember to speak clearly and slowly.

Don't worry if you make a mistake or forget a part of the joke - just keep going and have fun!

Pause at the punchline to build up suspense.

Always end your joke with a big smile and enjoy the laughter with your friends!

What do you call cheese that isn't yours?

Nacho cheese!

What do you call a pig that knows karate?

A pork chop!

Riddle

What starts with a T, ends with a T, and has T in it?

Answer

A teapot!

What is a rabbit's favorite kind of music?

Hip hop!

Why do bananas have to put on sunscreen before they go to the beach?

Because they might peel!

Riddle

What is yours but mostly used by others?

Answer

Your name

4

Why wouldn't the crab share his sweets?

Because he was a little shellfish!

What sound do porcupines make when they kiss?

Ouch!

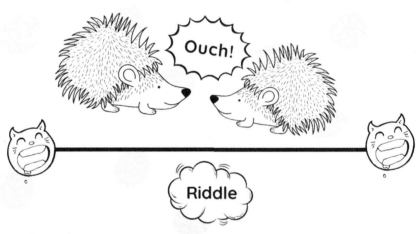

Riddle

I jump when I walk and sit when I stand. What am I?

Answer

Kangaroo

5

What did the baby laptop call her father?

Data!

Why was the cell phone scared to go to the dentist?

He didn't want them to remove his blue tooth!

Riddle

What has legs but doesn't walk?

Answer

A table

What do you call a cow on a trampoline?

A milk shake!

What do you call a sad strawberry?

A blueberry!

Riddle

What has hands but can't clap?

Answer

A clock

What is the most famous type of animal in the sea?

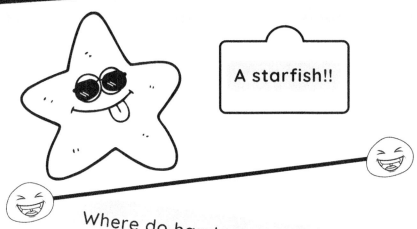

A starfish!!

Where do hamburgers go if they want to go dancing?

The meatball!

Riddle

I have no legs. I will never walk, but I always run.
What am I?

Answer

A river

Why couldn't the duck stop laughing?

He was quacking up!

What's the strongest type of sea creature?

Mussels!

Riddle

I have a dark side, and only a few people have stepped on me. I never stay full for long. What am I?

Answer

The moon.

Where do fish keep their money?

In the river bank!

What do you call a duck that gets good grades?

A wise quacker!

Riddle

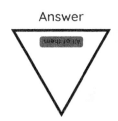

What month of the year has 28 days?

Answer

All of them.

Knock, knock.

Who's there?

Nobody.

Nobody who?

(Stay silent)

 ————————————

How do you make a tissue dance?

Put a little boogie in it!

What position does a ghost play in soccer?

The ghoulie!

How are false teeth like stars?

They come out at night.

What's worse than finding a worm in your apple?

Finding half a worm.

Riddle

What loses its head in the morning and gets it back at night?

Answer

A pillow

What's the difference between broccoli and boogers?

Kids don't eat broccoli!

Why can't an egg tell a joke?

It will crack up!

Riddle

What goes in a bird bath but never gets wet?

Answer

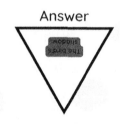

The bird's shadow

Why did the picture go to jail?

It was framed!

What did the zero say to the eight?

Nice belt!

0.....8 ?

Riddle

I'm light as a feather, yet the strongest person can't hold me for five minutes.
What am I?

Answer

Your breath

Where do you find a dog with no legs?

Right where you left him!

What do you call the horse that lives next door?

Your neighbor!

Riddle

I'm tall when I'm young and short when I'm old. What am I?

Answer

A candle

Why did the scientist wear denim?

Because he was a jean-ius.

Why did the chef get sent to prison?

Because he beat the eggs and whipped the cream.

Riddle

Which question can you never answer "yes" to?

Answer

Are you asleep?

What building has the most stories?

The library!

What did the pecan say to the walnut?

We are friends because we are both nuts!

Knock, knock,

Who's there?

Atch.

Atch who?

Bless you!

What kind of kitten works in a hospital?

A first-aid kit!

What did the little corn say to the mama corn?

POPCORN

Where is pop corn?

Riddle

What goes up but never comes down?

Answer

Your age

Knock, knock.

Who's there?

Little old lady.

Little old lady who?

I didn't know you could yodel!

What do you get when you cross a ball and a cat?

A fur ball.

What is a monster's favorite dessert?

I scream!

Where do sheep get their wool cut?

At the BAAAbars!

Why can't you trust a burrito?

OOPS!

Because it will spill the beans!

Riddle

If you drop me, I'm sure to crack but smile at me, and I'll smile back. What am I?

Answer

A mirror

20

What kind of room doesn't have doors?

A mushroom!

What do you call two banana peels?

A pair of slippers!

Riddle

What has a head and a tail but no body?

Answer

A coin

What kind of fruit do twins love the most?

Pears!

What's one way the moon cuts his hair?

Eclipse it!

Riddle

What's something that falls but will never hit the ground?

Answer

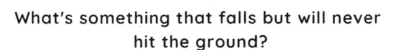

The temperature

What do you call an alligator in a vest?

An investigator!

What happens when cows refuse to be milked?

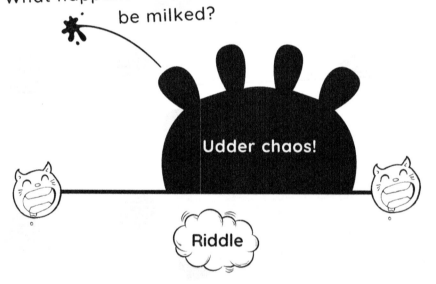

Udder chaos!

Riddle

I have cities but no houses. I have forests but no trees. I have water but no fish. What am I?

Answer

A map.

What did the big flower say to the little flower?

What's up, bud?

Why do beets always win?

They're un-BEET-able!

Riddle

What's something that, the more you take, the more you leave behind?

Answer

Footsteps

24

How do you organize a space party?

Planet early!

What is red and smells like blue paint?

Red paint.

Riddle

What can you break, even if you never pick it up or touch it?

Answer

A promise

Why did the starfish blush?

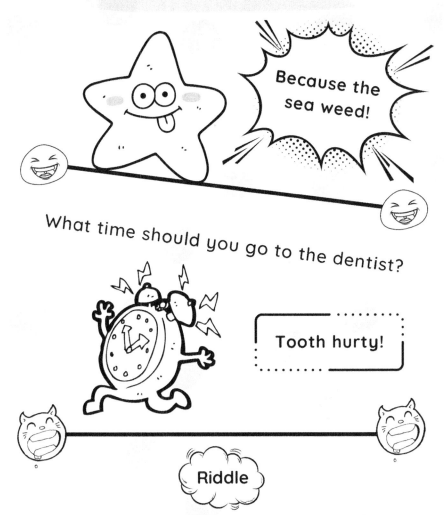

Because the sea weed!

What time should you go to the dentist?

Tooth hurty!

Riddle

Thanksgiving and Christmas are incomplete without me, and everyone tends to overeat when I'm on the table. What am I?

Answer

Why did the student eat his homework?

Because the teacher told him it was a piece of cake.

How do we know that the ocean is friendly?

It waves.

Hello!

Riddle

You can remove my skin, but I won't cry, but you might! What am I?

Answer

An onion.

What do you call a bear with no teeth?

A gummy bear!

What do kittens like to eat?

Mice cream!

Riddle

What does every birthday end with?

Answer

The letter Y

Do you want to hear a joke about pizza?

Never mind, it's too cheesy!

What do you call a gorilla with bananas in its ears?

Anything you like, he can't hear you!

Riddle

What can you catch but not throw?

Answer

A cold

What time is it when the clock strikes 13?

Time to get a new clock.

What do you call a dinosaur that is sleeping?

A dino-snore!

Riddle

Kate's mother has three children: Joe, James, and BLANK. Who is the third child?

Answer

Kate

What kind of music do balloons hate?

Pop music!

Why did the golfer wear two pairs of pants?

In case he got a hole-in-one!

Riddle

How many animals did Moses take on the ark?

Answer

Moses didn't take anything on the ark. Noah did.

What animal needs to wear a wig?

A bald eagle!

What do you call a magical dog?

A labra-cadabra-dor!

Riddle

What is as big as a cow but weighs nothing?

Answer

His shadow

Knock, knock.

Who's there?

Wooden shoe.

Wooden shoe who?

Wooden shoe like to know!

 ————————————

Why did the gum cross the road?

It was stuck to the chicken's foot!

 ————————————

What do you call a rich elf?

Welfy.

Knock, knock.

Who's there?

Interrupting cow.

Interrupting c...

MOO!!!

(Can be used with any animal. Just interrupt the other person with the animal noise!)

What do you call a fish with no eyes?

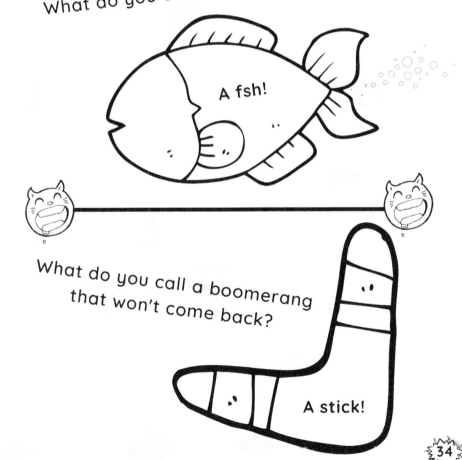

A fsh!

What do you call a boomerang that won't come back?

A stick!

What did the cat say when he fell off the table?

"Me-ow."

How do you make an octopus laugh?

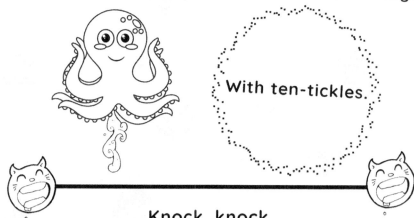

With ten-tickles.

Knock, knock.

Who's there?

Radio.

Radio who?

Radio not, here I come!

Knock, knock.

Who's there?

Lettuce.

Lettuce who?

Lettuce in, it's freezing out here!

What did one wall say to the other wall?

I'll meet you

at the corner!

Where do cows go for entertainment?

To the moooo-vies!

Why did the seagull fly over the sea?

Because if it flew over the bay, it would be a bagel!

What do snakes like to study in school?

Hissss-tory!

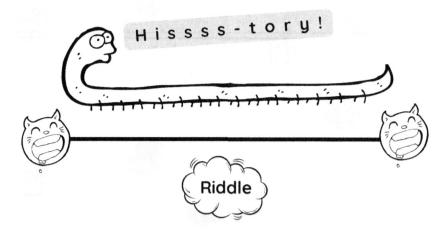

Riddle

I sometimes run, but I cannot walk. What am I?

Answer

Your nose

What do you call a story about a broken pencil?

Point-less!

What kind of tree fits in your hand?

A palm tree!

Riddle

What falls in winter but never gets hurt?

Answer

Knock, knock.

Who's there?

Stopwatch.

Stopwatch who?

Stopwatch you're doing and let me in!

 ———————————————

How did Cookie Monster feel after eating all the cookies?

Pretty crummy!

What do you give a sick lemon?

Lemon aid!

Knock, knock.

Who's there?

Harry.

Harry who?

Harry up and answer the door!

What do you call a sleeping bull?

A bull-dozer.

Why did the snake cross the road?

To get to the other sssssside!

Knock, knock.

Who's there?

Cows go.

Cows go who?

No, cows go MOO!

Why are ghosts bad liars?

Because you can see right through them!

What has four wheels and flies?

A garbage truck!

What is a cat's favorite color?

Purrr-ple.

Why don't pirates shower before they walk the plank?

Because they'll just wash up onshore later!

Knock, knock.

Who's there?

Dishes.

Dishes who?

Dishes the police, open up!

Why did the teddy bear not want any dessert?

Because she was stuffed!

Why did the math book look so sad?

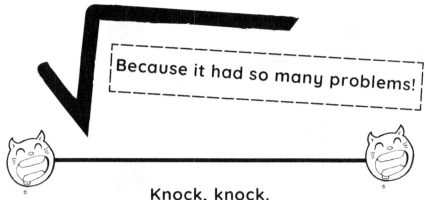

Because it had so many problems!

Knock, knock.

Who's there?

Figs.

Figs who?

Figs the doorbell. I've been knocking forever!

Why did the man put sugar on his pillow?

He wanted to have sweet dreams!

Why do bees have sticky hair?

Because they use honeycombs.

Knock, knock.

Who's there?

Ice cream.

Ice cream who?

Ice cream if you don't let me in!

Why didn't the skeleton go to school?

His heart wasn't in it!

What cat likes living in water?

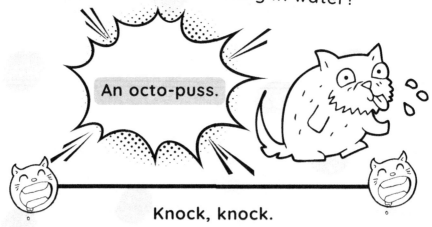

An octo-puss.

Knock, knock.

Who's there?

Woo.

Woo who?

Glad you're excited, too!

Knock, knock.

Who's there?

Boo.

Boo who?

Please don't cry. It's only a joke.

How do you make a lemon drop?

Just let go of it!

Why did the robber jump in the shower?

He wanted to make a
clean getaway.

What did the banana say to the dog?

Bananas can't talk.

Why does nobody talk to circles?

Because there's no point.

Knock, knock.

Who's there?

Dozen.

Dozen who?

Dozen anybody want to let me in?

What do cats always wear when they go to bed?

Paw-jamas!

Why did the puppy get great grades in class?

He was the teacher's pet!

Riddle

What has many keys but can't open any doors?

Answer

A piano.

When is it bad luck to be followed by a black cat?

When you're a mouse.

What did the tiger say to her cub on his birthday?

It's roar birthday.

Knock, knock.

Who's there?

Tennis.

Tennis who?

Tennis five plus five.

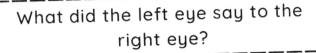

What did the left eye say to the right eye?

Between us, something smells.

Why is six afraid of seven?

Because seven eight nine.

Knock, knock.

Who's there?

Needle.

Needle who?

Needle little help opening the door!

Why did the cookie go to the hospital?

Because he felt crummy.

What kind of shoes do robbers wear?

Sneakers.

Riddle

There is one word spelled wrong in every English dictionary. What is it?

Answer

Wrong

Where would you take a sick boat?

To the dock!

Why did the teddy bear say no to dessert?

Because she was stuffed!

Riddle

What gets wetter and wetter the more it dries?

Answer

A towel!

What animal is always at a baseball game?

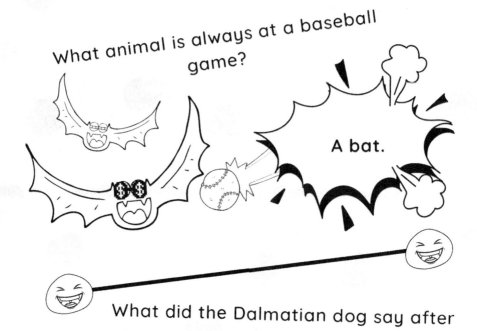

A bat.

What did the Dalmatian dog say after lunch?

That hit the spot.

Riddle

What can fill a room but doesn't take up space?

Answer

What does a cloud wear under his raincoat?

Thunderpants!

Why did the kid bring a ladder to school?

Because she wanted to go to high school!

Riddle

During which month do people sleep the least?

Answer

February (as February has fewer nights!)

Why did the kid cross the playground?

To get to the other slide!

What did one plate say to the other plate?

Dinner is on me!

Riddle

If you feed me, I grow, but if you give me water, I die. What am I?

Answer

Fire

What do you call a droid that takes the long way around?

R2 detour!

What did one volcano say to the other?

I lava you.

Riddle

What has legs but cannot walk?

Answer

A chair/table

Why did the toddler toss the butter out the window?

So she could see a butter-fly!

What do you call a cold dog?

A chili dog!

Riddle

What month of the year has 28 days?

Answer

All of them.

What do you get from a pampered cow?

Spoiled milk.

What did the ocean say to the pirate?

Nothing, it just waved.

Knock, knock.

Who's there?

Adore.

Adore who?

Adore is between you and me, so please open up!

What dinosaur had the best vocabulary?

The thesaurus!

Why did the banana go to the doctor?

Because it wasn't peeling well.

Riddle

What stays in the corner yet can travel all over the world?

Answer

A stamp

How do you stop an astronaut's baby from crying?

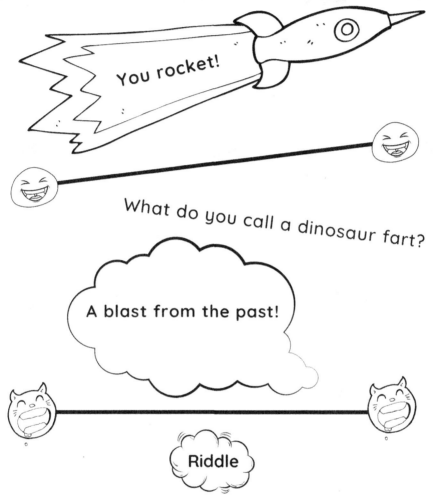

You rocket!

What do you call a dinosaur fart?

A blast from the past!

Riddle

I'm made of water, but if you put me into water, I die. What am I?

Answer

An ice cube.

How does a scientist freshen her breath?

With experi-mints!

Why are robots never afraid?

They have nerves of steel.

Riddle

What is always in front of you but can't be seen?

Answer

The future

What's a pirate's favorite country to travel to?

Arrrgh-entina!

What do you call a sheep that has no legs?

A cloud!

Riddle

What has a face and two hands, but no arms or legs?

Answer

A clock!

Why are fish so smart?

Because they live in schools!

What did the firefly say to her best friend?

"You glow, girl!"

Riddle

What two things can you never eat for breakfast?

Answer

Lunch and dinner.

Knock, knock

Who's there?

Me.

Me who?

Wow! Don't you know who you are?

 ————————————————

What did the mushroom say to the fungus?

You're a fun guy [fungi].

Why did the tomato blush?

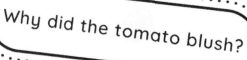

Because it saw the salad dressing!

What do you call a cow that plays the saxophone?

A moo-sician!

What's the most expensive fish called?

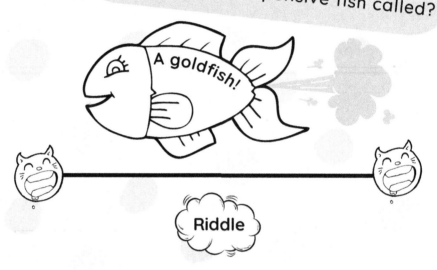

A goldfish!

Riddle

What is always in front of you but can't be seen?

Answer

The future

Did you hear about the guy who invented the knock-knock joke?

He won the "no-bell" prize!

Where do roses sleep at night?

In their flowerbed!

Riddle

What has a neck but no head and arms but no hands?

Answer

A shirt!

What did the traffic light say to the car?

Don't look.
I'm about to change!

What did the hat say to the head?

I've got you covered!

Riddle

What kind of band never plays music?

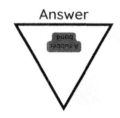

Answer

A rubber band

What is a tree's least favorite month of the year?

Sep-timber!

What candy is always running late to things?

Choco-late!

Knock knock.

Who's there?

Icy.

Icy who?

Icy you trying not to laugh at my knock-knock joke!

What type of snake ate all the desserts?

A pie-thon.

What candy do bumblebees love the most?

Bumble gum.

Riddle

What can you hold in your left hand but not in your right?

Answer

Your right elbow.

69

What do cats eat for breakfast?

Mice Krispies!

What type of shoes do frogs have too many pairs of?

Open-toad shoes!

Riddle

Which word becomes shorter when you add two letters to it?

Answer

The word short.

What kind of shoes do ninjas wear?

Sneakers!

Why did the motorcycle not want to go hiking?

Because he was two-tired!

Riddle

What's bright orange with green on top and sounds like a parrot?

Answer

A carrot

Why does Peter Pan fly around so much?

He Neverlands!

What's a pencil's favorite place to visit?

Pencil-vania!

Riddle

The more of this there is, the less you see.
What is it?

Answer

Darkness

What did the pig say on a hot day?

I'm bacon!

FART

How do billboards talk to each other?

With sign language!

Riddle

What needs to be broken before you can use it?

Answer

An egg.

Why didn't the duck pay for the lip balm?

He wanted to put it on his bill!

What did the Mom tomato say to the slow baby tomato?

"Ketchup."

Riddle

What can't talk but will reply when spoken to?

Answer

An echo

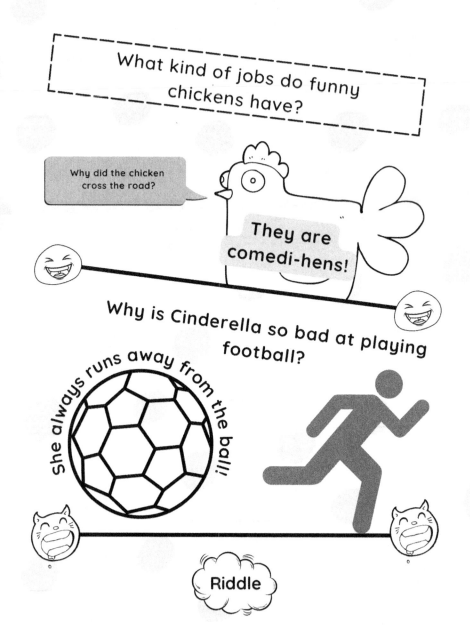

What kind of jobs do funny chickens have?

Why did the chicken cross the road?

They are comedi-hens!

Why is Cinderella so bad at playing football?

She always runs away from the ball!

Riddle

What has no life but can still die?

Answer

Why was the broom late?

It over-swept!

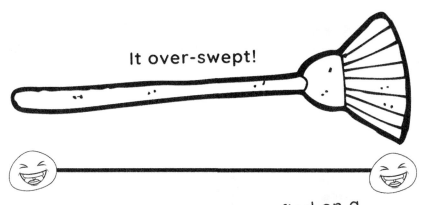

What kind of photos will you find on a turtle's phone?

Shell-fies!

Riddle

How many letters are there in the alphabet?

Answer

Eleven - T-h-e a-l-p-h-a-b-e-t

What's a pirate's favorite class to take in school?

Arrrrrt!

What do you get when you combine an elephant with a fish?

Swimming trunks!

Riddle

I make a loud sound when I'm changing. When I do change, I get bigger but weigh less. What am I?

Answer

Popcorn

What did the traffic light say to the car?

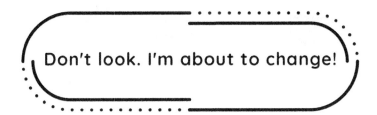

Don't look. I'm about to change!

Did you hear about the kidnapping in the park?

They woke him up!

Riddle

What type of cheese is made backward?

Answer

Edam

Which superhero is a pro at hitting home runs?

Batman!

What did Venus say while flirting with Saturn?

"Give me a ring sometime."

Riddle

You see me once in June, twice in November, and not at all in May. What am I?

Answer

The letter "e."

What was one of the first things
the elf learned in class?

The elf-abet!

What did the snowman say to the other
snowman?

Do you smell
carrots?

Riddle

Why would a man living in New York not
be buried in Chicago?

Answer

Because he is
still living!

What do you call a famous turtle?

A shell-ebrity

Why did the melon jump into the lake?

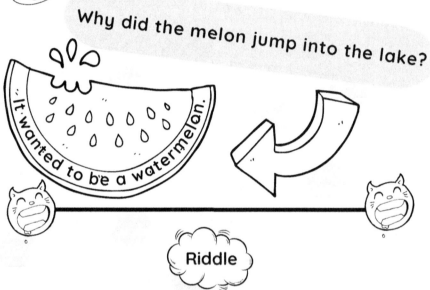

It wanted to be a watermelon.

Riddle

You will buy me to eat but never eat me.
What am I?

Answer

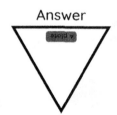

A plate

Why do people stop being a vegetarian?

It was a huge missed steak!

Did you get that joke about the ceiling?

Me neither. It was over my head!

Riddle

What kind of cup doesn't hold water?

Answer

A Cupcake (or hiccup!)

What do you call a medieval lamp?

Knight light!

What is a calendar's favourite food?

Dates!

Riddle

I'm round and have many layers, but if you get too close, I'll make you cry. What am I?

Answer

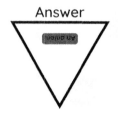

An onion

What kind of award do dentists hate to receive?

A plaque!

Why couldn't the NASA scientist get a room reservation on the moon?

It was full!

Riddle

You bought me for dinner but never ate me.
What am I?

Answer

cutlery

What is a robot's favorite snack?

Computer chips!

What did the husband pen say to the wife pen?

You're always write!

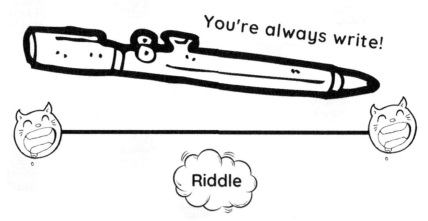

Riddle

What has a head, and a tail, is brown, and has no legs?

Answer

A penny

What does a vampire take for a sore throat?

Coffin drops!

Why did the cell phone get glasses?

Because she lost all her contacts!

Riddle

If you drop a yellow hat in the Red Sea, what does it become?

Answer

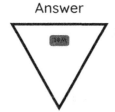

Why did Matt go out with a fig?

Because he couldn't get a date.

 ———————————————————————

What did the fisherman say to the magician?

Pick a cod, any cod.

Riddle

What is the last thing you take off before bed?

Answer

Your feet off the floor.

How does a vampire start a letter?

"Tomb it may concern..."

Where should you go if you want to learn how to make ice cream?

Sundae school!

Riddle

What is full of holes but still holds water?

Answer

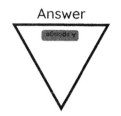

A sponge

Knock, knock.

Who's there?

Tank.

Tank who?

You're welcome!

 ———————————————————————

Why did the teacher put on sunglasses?

Because her students were so bright!

What do you call a dog that can tell time?

A watch dog!

Why is Santa good at karate?

He has a black belt.

Why did the turkey join a band?

So he could use his drumsticks!

Riddle

What has 1,000 legs and no feet?

Answer

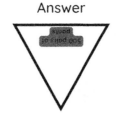

500 pairs of pants

Why did the frog take the bus to work today?

His car got toad away!

Have you heard the rumor about butter?

Nevermind, I shouldn't be spreading rumours!

Riddle

What goes in your pocket but keeps it empty?

Answer

A hole

What kind of key doesn't open locks?

A monkey!

Why was the traffic light late for his date?

It took him too long to change!

Riddle

What's really easy to get into and hard to get out of?

Answer

Trouble

Where does a sink go dancing?

The Dish-co!

What is corn's favorite music?

Pop!

Riddle

What do turtles, eggs, and beaches all have?

Answer

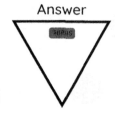

snails

What do you call a fake noodle?

An impasta!

What is an astronaut's favorite part on a computer?

The space bar!!

Riddle

I am a rock bigger than Venus but smaller than Uranus. What am I?

Answer

Earth

What did the shark say when he ate the clownfish?

This tastes a little funny!

What did the DNA say to the other DNA?

Do these genes make me look fat?

Riddle

How can a man go 8 days without sleep?

Answer

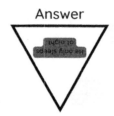

He only sleeps at night.

Why was the math book sad?

Because it had so many problems.

Why did the computer go to the doctor?

It had a virus!

What has a thumb and four fingers but is not alive?

Answer

A glove.

Where do polar bears vote?

At the North Pole!

What did the apple tree say to the farmer?

Stop picking on me!

Riddle

What gets sharper the more you use it?

Answer

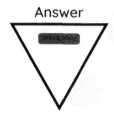

Your brain

What did the clock ask the watch?

Hour you doing?

What did the tree say to the wind?

Leaf me alone!

Riddle

If you drop a yellow hat in the Red Sea,
what does it become?

Answer

Wet

98

What does a spider wear to her wedding?

A webbing dress!

Why did the bird get in trouble in class?

Because he was caught tweeting on a test.

Riddle

When things go wrong, what can you always count on?

Answer

Your fingers

What did one pickle say to the other pickle who wouldn't stop complaining?

"Dill with it."

Why are ghosts bad liars?

Because you can see right through them!

Riddle

Give me air, and I will live. Give me water, and I will die. What am I?

Answer

How do you know when the moon has had enough to eat?

When it's full!

Where does the chicken like to eat?

At a rooster-ant!

Riddle

If you drop me, I'm sure to crack but smile at me, and I'll smile back. What am I?

Answer

A mirror

Why don't cats like online shopping?

They prefer a
cat-alogue!

Why are sports stadiums always so cool?

They are filled with fans!

Riddle

What has a neck but no head?

Answer

A bottle!

Thank you so much for your order.
You just made my business grow,
and for that, I am grateful!

If you enjoyed this book, please take
a few moments to leave a review.

For more hilarious jokes, check out the
hilarious joke book series!

Printed in Great Britain
by Amazon

22729402R00059